SHAKESPEARE'S LITTLE BOOK OF WISDOM

HarperCollins*Publishers*
1 London Bridge Street
London SE1 9GF
www.harpercollins.co.uk

First published by HarperCollins*Publishers* in 2016

1 3 5 7 9 10 8 6 4 2

Compiled by Steve King
Based on the Alexander Text, as per *The Complete Works of William Shakespeare* (Collins 1951, 2010)
Cover design by e-Digital Design
Cover image credit: Portrait of William Shakespeare, engraved by R. A. Artlett from the Chandos portrait © duncan1890 / iStock
Text design by e-Digital Design

A catalogue record for this book is available from the British Library

ISBN 978-0-00-795485-8

Printed in the United Kingdom

MIX

Paper from responsible sources

FSC™ C007454

FSC™ is a non-profit international organisation established to promote the responsible management of the world's forests. Products carrying the FSC label are independently certified to assure consumers that they come from forests that are managed to meet the social, economic and ecological needs of present and future generations, and other controlled sources.

Find out more about HarperCollins and the environment at
www.harpercollins.co.uk/green

SHAKESPEARE'S LITTLE BOOK OF WISDOM

Plays, Poetry and Sonnets

Compiled by Steve King

WILLIAM
COLLINS

Contents

A Note from the Compiler

In *As You Like It*, the forlorn figure of Jaques gives a famous speech in which he guides a group of his fellows through the Seven Ages of Man. The play is a comedy, focused on young lovers trying to find their place in a tumbling world, but, typical of Shakespeare, at the heart of it lies this disturbing reminder that our lives will ultimately come to a bleak end.

Shakespeare's work is full of this sort of sudden, unforeseen insight. He had a genius for underpinning his stories with the structure of how the world really works. The ill-fated

Romeo, we are reminded, may be truly in love, but he was besotted with another girl just days earlier. In *Hamlet,* that infuriating bureaucrat Polonius is also shown to be a caring father who can give his son valuable advice. Shakespeare's most tragic figure, King Lear, is not spared our laughter when ridiculed by a fool. In each of his plays, there are always such moments, where the scene in the foreground rolls back to reveal the whole pageant of human life behind.

I believe it is these moments that explain why Shakespeare remains so rewarding to us today,

400 years after his death. Not only are there thousands of lines filled with knowledge about life's rewards and hardships, but there is a recognition that this understanding might be glimpsed by anyone – not just by the great heroes, but by bit players, villains and fools, too.

At the beginning of the Ages of Man speech, Jaques informs the company punningly that 'All the world's a stage'. The play's first audience, standing in the Globe Theatre, must have grasped that those words were being spoken directly to them. Shakespeare knew that, beyond entertainment, the first purpose of drama is to hold a mirror up to our very nature. Gathered here in this little book are words of his wisdom on the 'many parts' that life will ask us to play.

SK, February 2016

Youth

When we are born, we cry that we are come
To this great stage of fools.

Lear, *King Lear*, Act IV, Scene 4

Youth

The world must be peopled.

Benedick, *Much Ado About Nothing,* Act II, Scene 3

It is a wise father that knows his own child.

Launcelot, *The Merchant of Venice*, Act II, Scene 2

Thou art thy mother's glass and she in thee
Calls back the lovely April of her prime;
So thou through windows of thine age shalt see,
Despite of wrinkles, this thy golden time.

Sonnet 3

Those that do teach young babes
Do it with gentle means and easy tasks.

Desdemona, *Othello*, Act IV, Scene 2

Be patient, for the world is broad and wide.

Friar Lawrence, *Romeo and Juliet,* Act III, Scene 3

Young blood doth not obey an old decree.

Berowne, *Love's Labour's Lost,* Act IV, Scene 3

Youth

Care keeps his watch in every old man's eye,
And where care lodges sleep will never lie;
But where unbruised youth with unstuff'd brain
Doth couch his limbs, there golden sleep
doth reign.

Friar Lawrence, *Romeo and Juliet,* Act II, Scene 3

How sharper than a serpent's tooth it is
To have a thankless child.

Lear, *King Lear,* Act I, Scene 4

Youth

The whining schoolboy, with his satchel
And shining morning face, creeping like snail
Unwillingly to school.

Jaques, *As You Like It,* Act II, Scene 7

Now 'tis the spring, and weeds are shallow rooted;
Suffer them now, and they'll o'ergrow the garden.

The Queen, *Henry VI, Part 2*, Act III, Scene 1

 Youth 

Youth to itself rebels, though none else near.

Laertes, *Hamlet*, Act I, Scene 3

Youth, the more it is wasted, the sooner it wears.

Falstaff, *Henry IV, Part 1*, Act II, Scene 4

 Youth 

We were, fair Queen,
Two lads that thought there was no more behind
But such a day to-morrow as to-day,
And to be boy eternal.

Polixenes, *The Winter's Tale,* Act I, Scene 2

Better a little chiding than a great deal of heart-break.

Mrs Page, *The Merry Wives of Windsor*, Act V, Scene 3

Youth

Every present time doth boast itself
Above a better gone.

Paulina, *The Winter's Tale,* Act V, Scene 1

Young men's love, then, lies
Not truly in their hearts, but in their eyes.

Friar Lawrence, *Romeo and Juliet*, Act II, Scene 3

Youth

The younger rises when the old doth fall.

Edmund, *King Lear*, Act III, Scene 3

Youth

Crabbed age and youth cannot live together:
Youth is full of pleasance, age is full of care;
Youth like summer morn, age like winter weather;
Youth like summer brave, age like winter bare:
Youth is full of sports, age's breath is short,
Youth is nimble, age is lame;
Youth is hot and bold, age is weak and cold,
Youth is wild, and age is tame.
Age, I do abhor thee; youth, I do adore thee;
O! my love, my love is young!
Age, I do defy thee.
O sweet shepherd, hie thee,
For methinks thou stay'st too long.

The Passionate Pilgrim, Stanza 12

Youth

I would there were no age between ten and three and twenty, or that youth would sleep out the rest; for there is nothing in the between but getting wenches with child, wronging the ancientry, stealing, fighting – Hark you now! Would any but these boiled brains of nineteen and two-and-twenty hunt this weather?

Shepherd, *The Winter's Tale*, Act III, Scene 3

Friendship

Love all, trust a few,
Do wrong to none; be able for thine enemy
Rather in power than use, and keep thy friend
Under thy own life's key.

Countess of Rousillon,
All's Well That Ends Well, Act I, Scene 1

Nature teaches beasts to know their friends.

Sicinius, *Coriolanus,* Act II, Scene 1

A friend should bear his friend's infirmities.

Cassius, *Julius Caesar*, Act IV, Scene 3

Neither a borrower nor a lender be;
For loan oft loses both itself and friend,
And borrowing dulls the edge of husbandry.

Polonius, *Hamlet,* Act I, Scene 3

We few, we happy few, we band of brothers;
For he to-day that sheds his blood with me
Shall be my brother.

The King, *Henry V*, Act IV, Scene 3

'There is flattery in friendship.'

Constable, *Henry V*, Act III, Scene 7

Misery acquaints a man with strange bedfellows.

Trinculo, *The Tempest,* Act II, Scene 2

I count myself in nothing else so happy
As in a soul rememb'ring my good friends;
And as my fortune ripens with thy love,
It shall be still thy true love's recompense.

Bolingbroke, *Richard II,* Act II, Scene 3

Do as adversaries do in law –
Strive mightily, but eat and drink as friends.

Tranio, *The Taming of the Shrew*, Act I, Scene 2

I myself am best
When least in company.

The Duke, *Twelfth Night,* Act I, Scene 4

This we prescribe, though no physician;
Deep malice makes too deep incision.
Forget, forgive; conclude and be agreed.

King Richard, *Richard II*, Act I, Scene 1

Those friends thou hast, and their adoption tried,
Grapple them unto thy soul with hoops of steel.

Polonius, *Hamlet,* Act I, Scene 3

Courage and Caution

Every man's conscience is a thousand men.

Oxford, *Richard III*, Act V, Scene 2

'Tis true we are in great danger.
The greater therefore should our courage be.

The King, *Henry V*, Act IV, Scene 1

Action is eloquence.

Volumnia, *Coriolanus,* Act III, Scene 2

Who dares not stir by day must walk by night.

The Bastard, *King John,* Act I, Scene 1

All things are ready, if our minds be so.

The King, *Henry V*, Act IV, Scene 3

'A fool's bolt is soon shot.'

Orleans, *Henry V*, Act II, Scene 7

Our doubts are traitors,
And make us lose the good we oft might win
By fearing to attempt.

Lucio, *Measure for Measure,* Act I, Scene 4

The fire in the flint
Shows not till it be struck.

Poet, *Timon of Athens,* Act I, Scene 1

Who seeks, and will not take when once 'tis offer'd,
Shall never find it more.

Menas, *Antony and Cleopatra,* Act II, Scene 7

Be bloody, bold, and resolute.

Second Apparition, *Macbeth,* Act IV, Scene 1

If you be afear'd to hear the worst,
Then let the worst, unheard, fall on your head.

The Bastard, *King John,* Act IV, Scene 2

Lions make leopards tame.

King Richard, *Richard II,* Act I, Scene 1

In the night, imagining some fear,
How easy is a bush suppos'd a bear?

Theseus, *A Midsummer Night's Dream,* Act V, Scene 1

Have more than thou showest,
Speak less than thou knowest,
Lend less than thou owest,
Ride more than thou goest,
Learn more than thou trowest,
Set less than thou throwest;
Leave thy drink and thy whore,
And keep in-a-door,
And thou shalt have more
Than two tens to a score.

Fool, *King Lear,* Act I, Scene 4

Since all is well, keep it so: wake not a sleeping wolf.

Chief Justice, *Henry IV, Part 2*, Act I, Scene 2

Beware
Of entrance to a quarrel; but being in,
Bear't that th' opposed may beware of thee.

Polonius, *Hamlet*, Act I, Scene 3

Screw your courage to the sticking place,
And we'll not fail.

Lady Macbeth, *Macbeth,* Act I, Scene 7

He must have a long spoon that must eat with the devil.

Dromio of Syracuse, *The Comedy of Errors*, Act IV, Scene 3

It is the bright day that brings forth the adder.

Brutus, *Julius Caesar*, Act II, Scene 1

Yield not thy neck
To fortune's yoke, but let thy dauntless mind
Still ride in triumph over all mischance.

Lewis, *Henry VI, Part 3,* Act III, Scene 3

If it were done when 'tis done, then 'twere well
It were done quickly.

Macbeth, *Macbeth*, Act I, Scene 7

If we are mark'd to die, we are enow
To do our country loss; and if to live,
The fewer men, the greater share of honour.

The King, *Henry V*, Act IV, Scene 3

When our actions do not,
Our fears do make us traitors.

Lady Macbeth, *Macbeth,* Act IV, Scene 2

The fox barks not when he would steal the lamb.

Suffolk, *Henry VI, Part 2,* Act III, Scene 1

Hold you still, I say.
Mine honour keeps the weather of my fate.
Life every man holds dear; but the dear man
Holds honour far more precious dear than life.

Hector, *Troilus and Cressida,* Act V, Scene 3

Be not afraid of shadows.

Ratcliff, *Richard III,* Act V, Scene 3

The fewer men, the greater share of honour.
We would not die in that man's company
That fears his fellowship to die with us.

The King, *Henry V*, Act IV, Scene 3

Present fears
Are less than horrible imaginings.

Macbeth, *Macbeth,* Act I, Scene 3

Out of this nettle, danger, we pluck this flower, safety.

Hotspur, *Henry IV, Part 1*, Act II, Scene 3

Oftentimes, to win us to our harm,
The instruments of darkness tell us truths,
Win us with honest trifles, to betray's
In deepest consequence.

Banquo, *Macbeth,* Act I, Scene 3

Now he'll outstare the lightning. To be furious
Is to be frighted out of fear, and in that mood
The dove will peck the estridge; and I see still
A diminution in our captain's brain
Restores his heart. When valour preys on reason,
It eats the sword it fights with.

Enobarbus, *Antony and Cleopatra,* Act III, Scene 13

Blind fear, that seeing reason leads, finds safer footing than blind reason stumbling without fear. To fear the worst oft cures the worse.

Cressida, *Troilus and Cressida,* Act III, Scene 2

I must go and meet with danger there,
Or it will seek me in another place
And find me worse provided.

Northumberland, *Henry IV, Part 2,* Act II, Scene 3

Honour pricks me on. Yea, but how if honour prick me off when I come on? How then? Can honour set to a leg? No. Or an arm? No. Or take away the grief of a wound? No. Honour hath no skill in surgery, then? No. What is honour? A word. What is in that word honour? Air. A trim reckoning! Who hath it? He that died o'Wednesday.

Falstaff, *Henry IV, Part 1*, Act V, Scene 1

Rumour doth double, like the voice and echo,
The numbers of the feared.

Warwick, *Henry IV, Part 2,* Act III, Scene 1

I have done enough. A lower place, note well,
May make too great an act; for learn this, Silius:
Better to leave undone than by our deed
Acquire too high a fame when him we serve's away.

Ventidius, *Antony and Cleopatra,* Act III, Scene 1

He which hath no stomach to this fight,
Let him depart; his passport shall be made,
And crowns for convoy put into his purse;
We would not die in that man's company
That fears his fellowship to die with us.

The King, *Henry V*, Act IV, Scene 3

Tempt not a desp'rate man.

Romeo, *Romeo and Juliet,* Act V, Scene 3

Good and Evil

If doing were as easy as to know what were good to do, chapels had been churches, and poor men's cottages princes' palaces.

Portia, *The Merchant of Venice*, Act I, Scene 2

Use them after your own honour and dignity. The less they deserve, the more merit is in your bounty.

Hamlet, *Hamlet,* Act II, Scene 2

I never did repent for doing good.

Portia, *The Merchant of Venice*, Act III, Scene 4

Few love to hear the sins they love to act.

Pericles, *Pericles,* Act I, Scene 1

A peace above all earthly dignities,
A still and quiet conscience.

The King, *Henry VIII,* Act III, Scene 3

I must be cruel only to be kind.

Hamlet, *Hamlet,* Act III, Scene 4

Wisdom and goodness to the vile seem vile.

Albany, *King Lear,* Act IV, Scene 2

Virtue finds no friends.

Queen Katharine, *Henry VIII,* Act III, Scene 1

They say best men are moulded out of faults;
And, for the most, become much more the better,
For being a little bad.

Mariana, *Measure for Measure,* Act V, Scene 1

If I lose mine honour,
I lose myself.

Antony, *Antony and Cleopatra*, Act III, Scene 4

How oft the sight of means to do ill deeds
Make deeds ill done!

King John, *King John,* Act IV, Scene 2

'Tis not enough to help the feeble up,
But to support him after.

Timon, *Timon of Athens*, Act I, Scene 1

There is some soul of goodness in things evil,
Would men observingly distil it out.

The King, *Henry V*, Act IV, Scene 1

The love of wicked men converts to fear,
That fear to hate.

King Richard, *Richard II,* Act V, Scene 1

The tempter or the tempted, who sins most?

Angelo, *Measure for Measure,* Act II, Scene 2

Kindness, nobler ever than revenge.

Oliver, *As You Like It,* Act IV, Scene 3

Suspicion always haunts the guilty mind.

Gloucester, *Henry VI, Part 3,* Act V, Scene 6

Virtue itself turns vice, being misapplied,
And vice sometime's by action dignified.

Friar Lawrence, *Romeo and Juliet,* Act II, Scene 3

Well, heaven forgive him! and forgive us all!
Some rise by sin, and some by virtue fall.

Escalus, *Measure for Measure*, Act II, Scene 1

The quality of mercy is not strain'd;
It droppeth as the gentle rain from heaven
Upon the place beneath. It is twice blest:
It blesseth him that gives and him that takes.

Portia, *The Merchant of Venice,* Act IV, Scene 1

O, benefit of ill; now I find true
That better is by evil still made better.

Sonnet 119

To do a great right, do a little wrong.

Bassanio, *The Merchant of Venice*, Act IV, Scene 1

Things ill got had ever bad success.

King Henry, *Henry VI, Part 3,* Act II, Scene 2

'Give the devil his due.'

Orleans, *Henry V*, Act II, Scene 7

Go to your bosom,
Knock there, and ask your heart what it doth know.

Isabella, *Measure for Measure,* Act II, Scene 2

There is no darkness but ignorance.

Clown, *Twelfth Night,* Act IV, Scene 2

Love and Romance

The course of true love never did run smooth.

Lysander, *A Midsummer Night's Dream,* Act I, Scene 1

Beauty is a witch
Against whose charms faith melteth into blood.

Claudio, *Much Ado About Nothing*, Act II, Scene 1

Words pay no debts, give her deeds.

Pandarus, *Troilus and Cressida,* Act V, Scene 3

Hasty marriage seldom proveth well.

Gloucester, *Henry VI, Part 3,* Act IV, Scene 1

I have no other but a woman's reason:
I think him so, because I think him so.

Lucetta, *The Two Gentlemen of Verona,* Act I, Scene 2

Love is a familiar; Love is a devil.
There is no evil angel but Love.

Armado, *Love's Labour's Lost,* Act I, Scene 2

'Who ever lov'd that lov'd not at first sight?'

Phebe, *As You Like It,* Act III, Scene 5

If music be the food of love, play on.
Give me excess of it, that, surfeiting,
The appetite may sicken and so die.

Orsino, *Twelfth Night*, Act I, Scene 1

Age cannot wither her, nor custom stale
Her infinite variety. Other women cloy
The appetites they feed, but she makes hungry
Where most she satisfies.

Enobarbus, *Antony and Cleopatra,* Act II, Scene 2

Love is blind, and lovers cannot see
The pretty follies that themselves commit.

Jessica, *A Midsummer Night's Dream*, Act I, Scene 1

To speak on the part of virginity is to accuse your mothers.

Parolles, *All's Well That Ends Well,* Act I, Scene 1

Good night, good night! Parting is such sweet sorrow
That I shall say good night till it be morrow.

Juliet, *Romeo and Juliet,* Act II, Scene 2

Lovers and madmen have such seething brains,
Such shaping fantasies, that apprehend
More than cool reason ever comprehends.
The lunatic, the lover, and the poet,
Are of imagination all compact.

Theseus, *A Midsummer Night's Dream,* Act V, Scene 1

Stony limits cannot hold love out,
And what love can do, that dares love attempt.

Romeo, *Romeo and Juliet,* Act II, Scene 2

Love is a spirit all compact of fire.

Venus and Adonis

Sigh no more, ladies, sigh no more,
Men were deceivers ever,
One foot in sea and one on shore,
To one thing constant never.

Balthasar, *Much Ado About Nothing*, Act II, Scene 3

Lovers ever run before the clock.

Gratiano, *The Merchant of Venice,* Act II, Scene 6

The hind that would be mated by the lion
Must die for love.

Helena, *All's Well That Ends Well,* Act I, Scene 1

The sight of lovers feedeth those in love.

Rosalind, *As You Like It,* Act III, Scene 4

There's beggary in the love that can be reckoned.

Antony, *Antony and Cleopatra*, Act I, Scene 1

Men have died from time to time, and worms have eaten them, but not for love.

Rosalind, *As You Like It,* Act IV, Scene 1

Let me not to the marriage of true minds
Admit impediments. Love is not love
Which alters when it alteration finds,
Or bends with the remover to remove.

Sonnet 116

To be wise and love
Exceeds man's might.

Cressida, *Troilus and Cressida,* Act III, Scene 2

Love looks not with the eyes, but with the mind;
And therefore is wing'd Cupid painted blind.

Helena, *A Midsummer Night's Dream,* Act I, Scene 1

Love goes toward love as school-boys from
their books;
But love from love, toward school with heavy looks.

Romeo, *Romeo and Juliet*, Act II, Scene 2

Love sought is good, but given unsought is better.

Olivia, *Twelfth Night,* Act III, Scene 1

What's mine is yours, and what is yours is mine.

The Duke, *Measure for Measure,* Act V, Scene 1

Therefore love moderately: long love doth so;
Too swift arrives as tardy as too slow.

Friar Lawrence, *Romeo and Juliet,* Act II, Scene 6

I grant I never saw a goddess go,
My mistress when she walks treads on
the ground.
And yet, by heaven, I think my love as rare
As any she belied with false compare.

Sonnet 130

He is the half part of a blessed man,
Left to be finished by such as she;
And she a fair divided excellence,
Whose fulness of perfection lies in him.
O, two such silver currents, when they join,
Do glorify the banks that bound them in;
And two such shores to two such streams
made one.

Citizens, *King John,* Act II, Scene 1

If men could be contented to be what they are, there were no fear in marriage.

Clown, *All's Well That Ends Well,* Act I, Scene 3

Our day of marriage shall be yours;
One feast, one house, one mutual happiness!

Valentine, *The Two Gentlemen of Verona,* Act V, Scene 4

Love's not Time's fool, though rosy lips
and cheeks
Within his bending sickle's compass come,
Love alters not with his brief hours and weeks,
But bears it out even to the edge of doom:
If this be error and upon me prov'd,
I never writ, nor no man ever lov'd.

Sonnet 116

You alone are you.

Sonnet 84

Work and Play

For some must watch, while some must sleep;
Thus runs the world away.

Hamlet, *Hamlet,* Act III, Scene 2

Things won are done; joy's soul lies in the doing.

Cressida, *Troilus and Cressida*, Act I, Scene 2

Talkers are no good doers.

First Murderer, *Richard III*, Act I, Scene 3

Experience is by industry achiev'd,
And perfected by the swift course of time.

Antonio, *The Two Gentlemen of Verona*, Act I, Scene 3

Better three hours too soon than a minute too late.

Ford, *The Merry Wives of Windsor*, Act II, Scene 2

When we mean to build,
We first survey the plot, then draw the model;
And when we see the figure of the house,
Then we must rate the cost of the erection;
Which if we find outweighs ability,
What do we then but draw anew the model
In fewer offices, or at least desist
To build at all?

Lord Bardolph, *Henry IV, Part 2*, Act I, Scene 3

He is well paid that is well satisfied.

Portia, *The Merchant of Venice*, Act IV, Scene 1

Sell when you can; you are not for all markets.

Rosalind, *As You Like It*, Act III, Scene 5

There is no virtue like necessity.

Gaunt, *Richard II,* Act I, Scene 2

To business that we love we rise betime
And go to't with delight.

Antony, *Antony and Cleopatra*, Act IV, Scene 4

Poor and content is rich, and rich enough;
But riches fineless is as poor as winter
To him that ever fears he shall be poor.

Iago, *Othello,* Act III, Scene 3

Delays have dangerous ends.

Alençon, *Henry VI, Part 1*, Act III, Scene 2

Small to greater matters must give way.

Lepidus, *Antony and Cleopatra,* Act II, Scene 2

Bait the hook well; this fish will bite.

Claudio, *Much Ado About Nothing*, Act II, Scene 2

When workmen strive to do better than well,
They do confound their skill in covetousness;
And oftentimes excusing of a fault
Doth make the fault the worse by th' excuse,
As patches set upon a little breach
Discredit more in hiding of the fault
Than did the fault before it was so patch'd.

Pembroke, *King John,* Act IV, Scene 2

The daintiest last, to make the end most sweet.

Bolingbroke, *Richard II*, Act I, Scene 3

Lack no discipline, make no delay;
For, lords, tomorrow is a busy day.

King Richard, *Richard III,* Act V, Scene 3

If all the year were playing holidays,
To sport would be as tedious as to work.

The Prince, *Henry VI, Part 1*, Act I, Scene 2

Good wine is a good familiar creature if it be well us'd.

Iago, *Othello*, Act II, Scene 3

It is a bawdy planet.

Leontes, *The Winter's Tale*, Act I, Scene 2

Mock the midnight bell.

Antony, *Antony and Cleopatra*, Act III, Scene 13

Wars and lechery! Nothing else holds fashion.

Thersites, *Troilus and Cressida,* Act II, Scene 3

'Tis ever common
That men are merriest when they are from home.

King Henry, *Henry V*, Act I, Scene 2

Dost thou think, because thou art virtuous, there shall be no more cakes and ale?

Sir Toby Belch, *Twelfth Night*, Act III, Scene 4

Life and Time

Come, madam wife, sit by my side and let the world slip; we shall ne'er be younger.

Sly, *The Taming of the Shrew*, Induction, Scene 2

Rough winds do shake the darling buds of May.
And summer's lease hath all too short a date.

Sonnet 18

The web of our life is of a mingled yarn, good and ill together. Our virtues would be proud if our faults whipt them not; and our crimes would despair if they were not cherish'd by our virtues.

Second Lord, *All's Well That Ends Well*, Act IV, Scene 3

Our loves and comforts should increase
Even as our days do grow!

Desdemona, *Othello*, Act II, Scene 1

There's a divinity that shapes our ends,
Rough-hew them how we will.

Hamlet, *Hamlet,* Act V, Scene 2

Why should a man whose blood is warm within
Sit like his grandsire cut in alabaster.

Gratiano, *The Merchant of Venice,* Act I, Scene 1

From hour to hour, we ripe and ripe,
And then, from hour to hour, we rot and rot;
And thereby hangs a tale.

Jaques, *As You Like It,* Act II, Scene 7

Farewell, a long farewell, to all my greatness!
This is the state of man: to-day he puts forth
The tender leaves of hopes; to-morrow blossoms
And bears his blushing honours thick upon him;
The third day comes a frost, a killing frost,
And when he thinks, good easy man, full surely
His greatness is a-ripening, nips his root,
And then he falls.

Wolsey, *Henry VIII,* Act III, Scene 2

The cat will mew, and dog will have his day.

Hamlet, *Hamlet,* Act V, Scene 1

Thus sometimes hath the brightest day a cloud,
And after summer evermore succeeds
Barren winter, with his wrathful nipping cold;
So cares and joys abound, as seasons fleet.

Gloucester, *Henry VI, Part 2*, Act II, Scene 4

The enemy increaseth every day:
We, at the height, are ready to decline.
There is a tide in the affairs of men
Which, taken at the flood, leads on to fortune;
Omitted, all the voyage of their life
Is bound in shallows and in miseries.
On such a full sea are we now afloat,
And we must take the current when it serves,
Or lose our ventures.

Brutus, *Julius Caesar,* Act IV, Scene 3

Though I now be old, and of the peace, if I see a sword out, my finger itches to make one. Though we are justices, and doctors, and churchmen, Master Page, we have some salt of our youth in us.

Shallow, *The Merry Wives of Windsor,* Act II, Scene 3

Not so young, sir, to love a woman for singing, nor so old to dote on her for anything. I have years on my back forty-eight.

Kent, *King Lear,* Act I, Scene 4

Men shut their doors against a setting sun.

Apemantus, *Timon of Athens,* Act II, Scene 1

 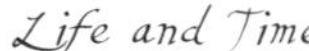

Life's but a walking shadow, a poor player
That struts and frets his hour upon the stage
And then is heard no more. It is a tale
Told by an idiot, full of sound and fury,
Signifying nothing.

Macbeth, *Macbeth*, Act V, Scene 5

There is a history in all men's lives,
Figuring the natures of the times deceas'd;
The which observ'd, a man may prophesy,
With a near aim, of the main chance of things
As yet not come to life, who in their seeds
And weak beginning lie intreasured.
Such things become the hatch and brood of time.

Warwick, *Henry IV, Part 2*, Act III, Scene 1

Tomorrow, and tomorrow, and tomorrow,
Creeps in this petty pace from day to day
To the last syllable of recorded time,
And all our yesterdays have lighted fools
The way to dusty death. Out, out, brief candle!

Macbeth, *Macbeth,* Act V, Scene 5

They say an old man is twice a child.

Rosencrantz, *Hamlet,* Act II, Scene 2

At Christmas I no more desire a rose
Than wish a snow in May's new-fangled shows;
But like of each thing that in season grows.

Berowne, *Love's Labour's Lost,* Act I, Scene 1

By heaven, it is as proper to our age
To cast beyond ourselves in our opinions
As it is common for the younger sort
To lack discretion.

Polonius, *Hamlet,* Act II, Scene 1

If to be old and merry be a sin, then many an old host that I know is damn'd.

Falstaff, *Henry IV, Part 1*, Act II, Scene 4

All is whole;
Not one word more of the consumed time.
Let's take the instant by the forward top;
For we are old, and on our quick'st decrees
Th' inaudible and noiseless foot of Time
Steals ere we can effect them.

The King, *All's Well That Ends Well,* Act V, Scene 3

I could be well content
To entertain the lag-end of my life
With quiet hours.

Worcester, *Henry IV, Part 1*, Act V, Scene 1

O gentlemen, the time of life is short!

Hotspur, *Henry IV, Part 1*, Act V, Scene 2

Power and Ambition

Greatness knows itself.

Hotspur, *Henry VI, Part 1*, Act IV, Scene 3

Glory is like a circle in the water,
Which never ceaseth to enlarge itself
Till by broad spreading it disperse to nought.

Pucelle, *Henry VI, Part 1*, Act I, Scene 1

We cannot all be masters.

Iago, *Othello*, Act I, Scene 1

To be thus is nothing,
But to be safely thus.

Macbeth, *Macbeth,* Act III, Scene 1

O, it is excellent
To have a giant's strength! But it is tyrannous
To use it like a giant.

Isabella, *Measure for Measure*, Act II, Scene 2

He that is proud eats up himself. Pride is his own glass, his own trumpet, his own chronicle; and whatever praises itself but in the deed devours the deed in the praise.

Agamemnon, *Troilus and Cressida*, Act II, Scene 2

Madness in great ones must not unwatch'd go.

King, *Hamlet,* Act V, Scene 2

New-made honour doth forget men's names.

The Bastard, *King John*, Act I, Scene 1

O, beware, my lord, of jealousy!
It is the green-eyed monster, which doth mock
The meat it feeds on.

Iago, *Othello*, Act III, Scene 3

Things sweet to taste prove in digestion sour.

Gaunt, *Richard II,* Act I, Scene 2

'Tis time to fear when tyrants seem to kiss.

Pericles, *Pericles*, Act I, Scene 2

The painful warrior famoused for fight,
After a thousand victories once foil'd,
Is from the book of honour razed quite,
And all the rest forgot for which he toil'd.

Sonnet 25

Nought's had, all's spent,
Where our desire is got without content.
'Tis safer to be that which we destroy
Than by destruction dwell in doubtful joy.

Lady Macbeth, *Macbeth*, Act III, Scene 2

What needs these feasts, pomps, and vainglories?

Apemantus, *Timon of Athens*, Act I, Scene 2

There is no sure foundation set on blood,
No certain life achiev'd by others' death.

King John, *King John,* Act IV, Scene 2

That lowliness is young ambition's ladder,
Whereto the climber-upward turns his face;
But when he once attains the upmost round,
He then unto the ladder turns his back,
Looks in the clouds, scorning the base degrees
By which he did ascend.

Brutus, *Julius Caesar*, Act II, Scene 1

Violent fires soon burn out themselves;
Small showers last long, but sudden storms
are short.

Gaunt, *Richard II*, Act II, Scene 1

Everything includes itself in power,
Power into will, will into appetite;
And appetite, an universal wolf,
So doubly seconded with will and power,
Must make perforce an universal prey,
And last eat up himself.

Ulysses, *Troilus and Cressida,* Act I, Scene 3

'If this fall into thy hand, revolve. In my stars I am above thee; but be not afraid of greatness. Some are born great, some achieve greatness, and some have greatness thrust upon 'em. Thy Fates open their hands; let thy blood and spirit embrace them.'

Malvolio, *Twelfth Night,* Act II, Scene 5

Gives not the hawthorn bush a sweeter shade
To shepherds looking on their silly sheep,
Than doth a rich embroider'd canopy
To kings that fear their subjects' treachery?

The King, *Henry IV, Part 2*, Act III, Scene 5

To guard a title that was rich before,
To gild refined gold, to paint the lily,
To throw a perfume on the violet,
To smooth the ice, or add another hue
Unto the rainbow, or with taper-light
To seek the beauteous eye of heaven to garnish,
Is wasteful and ridiculous excess.

Salisbury, *King John*, Act IV, Scene 2

Vaulting ambition, which o'erleaps itself
And falls on the other.

Macbeth, *Macbeth,* Act I, Scene 7

Too famous to live long!

Bedford, *Henry VI, Part 1*, Act I, Scene 1

He tires betimes that spurs too fast betimes;
With eager feeding food doth choke the feeder;
Light vanity, insatiate cormorant,
Consuming means, soon preys upon itself.

Gaunt, *Richard II,* Act II, Scene 1

How quickly nature falls into revolt
When gold becomes her object!

The King, *Henry IV, Part 2,* Act IV, Scene 5

Small things make base men proud.

Suffolk, *Henry VI, Part 2,* Act IV, Scene 1

'Tis mad idolatry
To make the service greater than the god.

Hector, *Troilus and Cressida,* Act II, Scene 2

Be advis'd:
Heat not a furnace for your foe so hot
That it do singe yourself.

Norfolk, *Henry VIII,* Act I, Scene 1

Uneasy lies the head that wears a crown.

The King, *Henry VI, Part 2,* Act III, Scene 1

The abuse of greatness is when it disjoins
Remorse from power.

Brutus, *Julius Caesar,* Act II, Scene 1

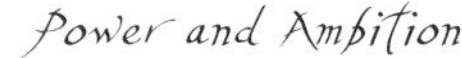

The patient dies while the physician sleeps;
The orphan pines while the oppressor feeds;
Justice is feasting while the widow weeps;
Advice is sporting while infection breeds:
Thou grant'st no time for charitable deeds:
Wrath, envy, treason, rape, and murder's rages,
Thy heinous hours wait on them as their pages.

The Rape of Lucrece

The very substance of the ambitious is merely the shadow of a dream.

Guildenstern, *Hamlet,* Act II, Scene 2

Theatre and the Arts

O for a Muse of fire, that would ascend
The brightest heaven of invention,
A kingdom for a stage, princes to act,
And monarchs to behold the swelling scene!

Chorus, *Henry V*, Prologue

Brevity is the soul of wit.

Polonius, *Hamlet,* Act II, Scene 2

My library
Was dukedom large enough.

Prospero, *The Tempest,* Act I, Scene 2

Where is any author in the world
Teaches such beauty as a woman's eye?

Berowne, *Love's Labour's Lost,* Act IV, Scene 3

The truest poetry is the most feigning, and lovers are given to poetry; and what they swear in poetry may be said as lovers they do feign.

Touchstone, *As You Like It,* Act III, Scene 3

The play's the thing
Wherein I'll catch the conscience of the King.

Hamlet, *Hamlet,* Act II, Scene 2

As in a theatre the eyes of men
After a well-grac'd actor leaves the stage
Are idly bent on him that enters next,
Thinking his prattle to be tedious.

York, *Richard II,* Act V, Scene 2

More matter, with less art.

The Queen, *Hamlet,* Act II, Scene 2

I hold the world but as the world, Gratiano –
A stage, where every man must play a part,
And mine a sad one.

Antonio, *The Merchant of Venice,* Act I, Scene 1

Theatre and the Arts

To see sad sights moves more than hear them told.

The Rape of Lucrece

Let your own discretion be your tutor. Suit the action to the word, the word to the action; with this special observance, that you o'erstep not the modesty of nature.

Hamlet, *Hamlet,* Act III, Scene 2

A jest's prosperity lies in the ear
Of him that hears it, never in the tongue
Of him that makes it.

Rosaline, *Love's Labour's Lost,* Act V, Scene 2

'Better a witty fool than a foolish wit.'

Clown, *Twelfth Night,* Act I, Scene 5

No epilogue, I pray you; for your play needs no excuse.

Theseus, *A Midsummer Night's Dream*, Act V, Scene 1

O sir, we quarrel in print by the book; as you have books for good manners: I will name you the degrees. The first, the Retort Courteous; the second, the Quip Modest; the third, the Reply Churlish; the fourth, the Reproof Valiant; the fifth, the Countercheque Quarrelsome; the sixth, the Lie with Circumstance; the seventh, the Lie Direct.

All these you may avoid but the Lie Direct; and you may avoid that too, with an If. I knew when seven justices could not take up a quarrel, but when the parties were met themselves, one of them thought but of an If, as: 'If you said so, then I said so;' and they shook hands and swore brothers. Your If is the only peacemaker; much virtue in If.

Touchstone, *As You Like It,* Act V, Scene 4

An honest tale speeds best being plainly told.

Queen Elizabeth, *Richard III*, Act IV, Scene 4

If we shadows have offended,
Think but this, and all is mended,
That you have but slumb'red here
While these visions did appear.
And this weak and idle theme,
No more yielding but a dream,
Gentles, do not reprehend.
If you pardon, we will mend.

Puck, *A Midsummer Night's Dream,* Act V, Scene 1

Truth and Appearances

What's aught but as 'tis valued?

Troilus, *Troilus and Cressida,* Act I, Scene 2

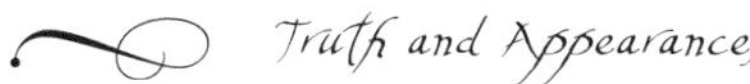

All hoods make not monks.

Queen Katharine, *Henry VIII,* Act III, Scene 1

Rumour is a pipe
Blown by surmises, jealousies, conjectures.

Rumour, *Henry IV, Part 2*, Induction

Truth is truth
To th' end of reck'ning.

Isabella, *Measure for Measure,* Act V, Scene 1

'All that glisters is not gold,'

The Prince of Morocco, *The Merchant of Venice*, Act II, Scene 8

There's no art
To find the mind's construction in the face.

Duncan, *Macbeth,* Act I, Scene 4

They say
every why hath a wherefore.

Dromio of Syracuse, *The Comedy of Errors,* Act II, Scene 2

Give every man thine ear, but few thy voice;
Take each man's censure, but reserve thy judgment.

Polonius, *Hamlet,* Act I, Scene 3

Knavery's plain face is never seen till used.

Iago, *Othello*, Act II, Scene 1

My crown is in my heart, not on my head;
Not deck'd with diamonds and Indian stones,
Not to be seen. My crown is call'd content;
A crown it is that seldom kings enjoy.

King Henry, *Henry VI, Part 3*, Act III, Scene 1

Good reasons must, of force, give place to better.

Brutus, *Julius Caesar*, Act IV, Scene 3

O, what may man within him hide,
Though angel on the outward side!

The Duke, *Measure for Measure,* Act III, Scene 2

The silence often of pure innocence
Persuades when speaking fails.

Paulina, *The Winter's Tale,* Act II, Scene 2

Reputation is an idle and most false imposition; oft got without merit and lost without deserving. You have lost no reputation at all, unless you repute yourself such a loser.

Iago, *Othello*, Act II, Scene 2

The will of man is by his reason sway'd,

Lysander, *A Midsummer Night's Dream,* Act II, Scene 2

Opinion's but a fool that makes us scan
The outward habit for the inward man.

Simonides, *Pericles,* Act II, Scene 2

Smooth runs the water where the brook is deep.

Suffolk, *Henry IV, Part 2,* Act III, Scene 1

Flattery is the bellows blows up sin.

Helicanus, *Pericles,* Act I, Scene 2

In the end truth will out.

Launcelot, *The Merchant of Venice,* Act II, Scene 2

Falser than vows made in wine.

Rosalind, *As You Like It,* Act II, Scene 5

My beauty, though but mean,
Needs not the painted flourish of your praise.

The Princess of France, *Love's Labour's Lost,* Act II, Scene 1

Through tatter'd clothes small vices do appear;
Robes and furr'd gowns hide all.

Lear, *King Lear,* Act IV, Scene 6

To be a well-favoured man is the gift of fortune.

Dogberry, *Much Ado About Nothing*, Act III, Scene 3

He that loves to be flattered is worthy o' th' flatterer.

Apemantus, *Timon of Athens*, Act I, Scene 1

Beauty itself doth of itself persuade
The eyes of men without an orator.

The Rape of Lucrece

Who knows himself a braggart,
Let him fear this; for it will come to pass
That every braggart will be found an ass.

Parolles, *All's Well That Ends Well,* Act IV, Scene 3

Truth loves open dealing.

Queen Katharine, *Henry VIII,* Act III, Scene 1

One may smile, and smile, and be a villain.

Hamlet, *Hamlet,* Act I, Scene 2

Ill-wind never said well.

Orleans, *Henry V*, Act II, Scene 7

Thought is free.

Stephano, *The Tempest*, Act III, Scene 2

The devil can cite Scripture for his purpose.

Antonio, *The Merchant of Venice,* Act I, Scene 3

Modest doubt is called
The beacon of the wise.

Hector, *Troilus and Cressida*, Act II, Scene 2

The empty vessel makes the greatest sound.

Boy, *Henry V*, Act IV, Scene 4

Though it be honest, it is never good
To bring bad news.

Cleopatra, *Antony and Cleopatra*, Act II, Scene 5

The world is still deceived with ornament.

Bassanio, *The Merchant of Venice*, Act III, Scene 4

Good counselors lack no clients.

Clown, *Measure for Measure,* Act I, Scene 2

Politics and Society

What is the city but the people?

Sicinius, *Coriolanus,* Act III, Scene 1

The self-same sun that shines upon his court
Hides not his visage from our cottage, but
Looks on alike.

Perdita, *The Winter's Tale,* Act IV, Scene 4

Whiles I am a beggar, I will rail
And say there is no sin but to be rich;
And being rich, my virtue then shall be
To say there is no vice but beggary.

The Bastard, *King John*, Act II, Scene 1

Know thou this, that men
Are as the time is.

Edmund, *King Lear,* Act V, Scene 3

It is an heretic that makes the fire,
Not she which burns in't.

Paulina, *The Winter's Tale*, Act II, Scene 3

No ceremony that to great ones longs,
Not the king's crown nor the deputed sword,
The marshal's truncheon nor the judge's robe,
Become them with one half so good a grace
As mercy does.

Isabella, *Measure for Measure,* Act II, Scene 2

Every subject's duty is the King's;
but every subject's soul is his own.

King Henry, *Henry V*, Act IV, Scene 1

They said they were an-hungry;
sigh'd forth proverbs –
That hunger broke stone walls,
that dogs must eat,
That meat was made for mouths,
that the gods sent not
Corn for the rich men only.

Marcius, *Coriolanus,* Act I, Scene 1

Those that with haste will make a mighty fire
Begin it with weak straws.

Cassius, *Julius Caesar*, Act I, Scene 3

Distribution should undo excess,
And each man have enough.

Gloucester, *King Lear,* Act IV, Scene 1

Therefore doth heaven divide
The state of man in divers functions
Setting endeavour in continual motion;
To which is fixed, as an aim or butt,
Obedience. So work the honey-bees,
Creatures that by a rule in nature teach
The act of order to a peopled kingdom.

Canterbury, *Henry V*, Act I, Scene 2

I this infer,
That many things, having full reference
To one consent, may work contrariously:
As many arrows, loosed several ways,
Come to one mark; as many ways meet
in one town;
As many fresh streams meet in one salt sea
As many lines close in the dial's centre;
So may a thousand actions, once afoot.
End in one purpose.

Canterbury, *Henry V*, Act I, Scene 2

Hardship and Hope

To be, or not to be – that is the question;
Whether 'tis nobler in the mind to suffer
The slings and arrows of outrageous fortune,
Or to take arms against a sea of troubles,
And by opposing end them?

Hamlet, *Hamlet,* Act III, Scene 1

As flies to wanton boys are we to th' gods.
They kill us for their sport.

Gloucester, *King Lear*, Act IV, Scene 1

Many men that stumble at the threshold
Are well foretold that danger lurks within.

Gloucester, *Henry VI, Part 3*, Act IV, Scene 7

Many can brook the weather that love not the wind.

Nathaniel, *Love's Labour's Lost,* Act IV, Scene 2

When sorrows come, they come not single spies.
But in battalions!

The King, *Hamlet*, Act IV, Scene 5

Where the greater malady is fix'd,
The lesser is scarce felt. Thou'dst shun a bear;
But if thy flight lay toward the roaring sea,
Thou'dst meet the bear i' th' mouth.

Lear, *King Lear,* Act III, Scene 4

Some griefs are med'cinable.

Imogen, *Cymbeline,* Act III, Scene 2

Things without all remedy
Should be without regard. What's done is done.

Lady Macbeth, *Macbeth*, Act III, Scene 2

Care is no cure, but rather corrosive,
For things that are not to be remedied.

La Pucelle, *Henry VI, Part 1*, Act III, Scene 3

The robbed that smiles, steals something from the thief.

The Duke, *Othello*, Act I, Scene 3

There's small choice in rotten apples.

Hortensio, *The Taming of the Shrew*, Act I, Scene 1

The strawberry grows underneath the nettle.

Ely, *Henry V*, Act I, Scene 1

We, ignorant of ourselves,
Beg often our own harms, which the wise pow'rs
Deny us for our good; so find we profit
By losing of our prayers.

Menecrates, *Antony and Cleopatra,* Act II, Scene 1

GAUNT. What is six winters? They are quickly gone.
BOLINGBROKE. To men in joy; but grief makes one hour ten.

Richard II, Act I, Scene 3

The worst is not
So long as we can say 'This is the worst.'

Edgar, *King Lear*, Act IV, Scene 1

Bear a fair presence, though your heart be tainted.

Luciana, *The Comedy of Errors,* Act III, Scene 2

Our remedies oft in ourselves do lie,
Which we ascribe to heaven.

Helena, *All's Well That Ends Well,* Act I, Scene 1

Come what come may,
Time and the hour runs through the roughest day.

Macbeth, *Macbeth,* Act I, Scene 3

For honour travels in a strait so narrow –
Where one but goes abreast. Keep then the path,
For emulation hath a thousand sons
That one by one pursue; if you give way,
Or hedge aside from the direct forthright,
Like to an ent'red tide they all rush by
And leave you hindmost.

Ulysses, *Troilus and Cressida*, Act III, Scene 3

Past and to come seems best; things present, worst.

Archbishop, *Henry IV, Part 2,* Act I, Scene 3

In cases of defense, 'tis best to weigh
The enemy more mighty than he seems.

Dauphin, *Henry V*, Act II, Scene 4

Some innocents scape not the thunderbolt.

Cleopatra, *Antony and Cleopatra,* Act II, Scene 5

Fortune brings in some boats that are not steer'd.

Pisanio, *Cymbeline,* Act IV, Scene 3

Men at some time are masters of their fates;
The fault, dear Brutus, is not in our stars,
But in ourselves.

Cassius, *Julius Caesar*, Act I, Scene 2

The end crowns all,
And that old common arbitrator, Time,
Will one day end it.

Hector, *Troilus and Cressida,* Act IV, Scene 5

What's past is prologue, what to come
In yours and my discharge.

Antonio, *The Tempest*, Act II, Scene 1

Death and Sorrow

Death –
The undiscover'd country, from whose bourn
No traveller returns.

Hamlet, *Hamlet,* Act III, Scene 1

Give sorrow words. The grief that does not speak
Whispers the o'erfraught heart and bids it break.

Malcolm, *Macbeth,* Act IV, Scene 3

A great reckoning in a little room.

Touchstone, *As You Like It,* Act III, Scene 3

All that lives must die,
Passing through nature to eternity.

The Queen, *Hamlet*, Act I, Scene 2

The dead are well.

Cleopatra, *Antony and Cleopatra,* Act II, Scene 5

The old bees die, the young possess their hive.

The Rape of Lucrece

The evil that men do lives after them;
The good is oft interred with their bones.

Antony, *Julius Caesar,* Act III, Scene 2

If thou and nature can so gently part,
The stoke of death is as a lover's pinch,
Which hurts and is desired.

Cleopatra, *Antony and Cleopatra*, Act V, Scene 2

Fear no more the heat o' the sun,
Nor the furious winter's rages;
Thou thy worldly task hast done,
Home art gone, and ta'en thy wages.
Golden lads and girls all must,
As chimney-sweepers, come to dust.

Guiderius, *Cymbeline,* Act IV, Scene 2

Fear no more the frown o' the great,
Thou art past the tyrant's stroke.
Care no more to clothe and eat;
To thee the reed is as the oak.
The sceptre, learning, physic, must
All follow this, and come to dust.

Arviragus, *Cymbeline,* Act IV, Scene 2

All lovers young, all lovers must
Consign to thee, and come to dust.

Guiderius and Arviragus, *Cymbeline,* Act IV, Scene 2

To weep is to make less the depth of grief.

Richard, *Henry VI, Part 3,* Act II, Scene 1

Cowards die many times before their deaths:
The valiant never taste of death but once.
Of all the wonders that I yet have heard,
It seems strange to me most strange that men
should fear,
seeing that death, a necessary end,
Will come when it will come.

Caesar, *Julius Caesar,* Act II, Scene 2

Make death proud to take us.

Cleopatra, *Antony and Cleopatra,* Act IV, Scene 15

Men must endure
Their going hence, even as their coming hither:
Ripeness is all.

Edgar, *King Lear,* Act V, Scene 2

The ground that gave them first has them again.
Their pleasures here are past, so is their pain.

Belarius, *Cymbeline,* Act IV, Scene 2

Why, what is pomp, rule, reign,
but earth and dust?
And, live we how we can, yet die we must.

Warwick, *Henry IV, Part 3*, Act V, Scene 2

What wound did ever heal but by degrees?

Iago, *Othello*, Act II, Scene 3

Praising what is lost
Makes the remembrance dear.

The King, *All's Well That Ends Well*, Act V, Scene 2

To die, to sleep;
To sleep, perchance to dream. Ay, there's the rub;
For in that sleep of death what dreams may come,
When we have shuffled off this mortal coil,
Must give us pause.

Hamlet, *Hamlet,* Act III, Scene 1

He that dies pays all debts.

Stephano, *The Tempest,* Act III, Scene 2

Let us not burden our remembrances with
A heaviness that's gone.

Prospero, *The Tempest,* Act V, Scene 1

Every one can master a grief but he that has it.

Benedick, *Much Ado About Nothing*, Act III, Scene 2

I find I seek to die
And seeking death, find life.

Claudio, *Measure for Measure,* Act III, Scene 1

Nothing can we call our own but death.

King Richard, *Richard II,* Act III, Scene 2

There is a special providence in the fall of a sparrow. If it be now, 'tis not to come; if it be not to come, it will be now; if it be not now, yet it will come – the readiness is all. Since no man knows aught of what he leaves, what is't to leave betimes? Let be.

Hamlet, *Hamlet*, Act V, Scene 2

Human Nature

What a piece of work is a man! How noble in reason! how infinite in faculties! in form and moving, how express and admirable! in action, how like an angel! in apprehension, how like a god! the beauty of the world! the paragon of animals! And yet, to me, what is this quintessence of dust? Man delights not me – no, nor woman neither.

Hamlet, *Hamlet,* Act II, Scene 2

Be to yourself
As you would to your friend.

Norfolk, *Henry VIII*, Act I, Scene 1

A man may fish with the worm that hath eat of a king, and eat of the fish that hath fed of that worm.

Hamlet, *Hamlet,* Act IV, Scene 3

Nature must obey necessity.

Brutus, *Romeo and Juliet,* Act IV, Scene 3

Men are men; the best sometimes forget.

Iago, *Othello,* Act II, Scene 3

The rain it raineth every day.

Fool, *King Lear,* Act III, Scene 2

For 'tis the mind that makes the body rich.

Petruchio, *The Taming of the Shrew*, Act IV, Scene 3

There was never yet philosopher
That could endure the toothache patiently.

Leonato, *Much Ado About Nothing*, Act V, Scene 1

What is a man,
If his chief good and market of his time
Be but to sleep and feed? A beast, no more!

Hamlet, *Hamlet,* Act IV, Scene 4

There is nothing either good or bad but thinking makes it so.

Hamlet, *Hamlet,* Act II, Scene 2

Silence is the perfectest herald of joy: I were but little happy if I could say how much.

Claudio, *Much Ado About Nothing*, Act II, Scene 1

All things that are
Are with more spirit chased than enjoyed.

Gratiano, *The Merchant of Venice,* Act II, Scene 6

Every thing that grows
Holds in perfection but a little moment.

Sonnet 15

There is occasions and causes why and wherefore in all things.

Fluellen, *Henry V*, Act V, Scene 1

We know what we are, but know not what we may be.

Ophelia, *Hamlet,* Act IV, Scene 5

What's in a name? That which we call a rose
By any other name would smell as sweet.

Juliet, *Romeo and Juliet*, Act II, Scene 2

But whate'er I be,
Nor I, nor any man that but man is,
With nothing shall be pleas'd till he be eas'd
With being nothing.

King Richard, *Richard II*, Act V, Scene 5

But man, proud man,
Dress'd in a little brief authority,
Most ignorant of what he's most assured,
His glassy essence, like an angry ape,
Plays such fantastic tricks before high heaven
As make the angels weep.

Isabella, *Measure for Measure*, Act II, Scene 2

Foolery, sir, does walk about the orb like the sun – it shines everywhere.

Clown, *Twelfth Night*, Act III, Scene 1

I am I, howe'er I was begot.

The Bastard, *King John,* Act I, Scene 1

Who riseth from a feast
With that keen appetite that he sits down?

Gratiano, *The Merchant of Venice,* Act II, Scene 6

Who can be wise, amaz'd, temp'rate,
and furious,
Loyal and neutral, in a moment? No man.

Macbeth, *Macbeth,* Act II, Scene 3

Our bodies are gardens to the which our wills are gardeners.

Iago, *Othello,* Act I, Scene 3

What fools these mortals be!

Puck, *A Midsummer Night's Dream,* Act III, Scene 2

I cannot tell; things must be as they may. Men may sleep, and they may have their throats about them at that time; and some say knives have edges. It must be as it may; though patience be a tired mare, yet she will plod. There must be conclusions. Well, I cannot tell.

Nym, *Henry V,* Act II, Scene 1

This above all – to thine own self be true,
And it must follow, as the night the day,
Thou canst not then be false to any man.

Polonius, *Hamlet,* Act I, Scene 3

We are not all alone unhappy:
This wide and universal theatre
Presents more woeful pageants than the scene
Wherein we play in.

Duke Senior, *As You Like It*, Act II, Scene 7

In nature there's no blemish but the mind.

Antonio, *Twelfth Night,* Act III, Scene 4

Conscience does make cowards of us all.

Hamlet, *Hamlet,* Act III, Scene 1

All the world's a stage,
And all the men and women merely players;
They have their exits and their entrances;
And one man in his time plays many parts.

Jaques, *As You Like It,* Act II, Scene 7

Nothing can come of nothing.
Nothing will come of nothing.

Lear, *King Lear,* Act I, Scene 1

Wisely and slow; they stumble that run fast.

Friar Lawrence, *Romeo and Juliet*, Act II, Scene 3

We are such stuff
As dreams are made on; and our little life
Is rounded with a sleep.

Prospero, *The Tempest,* Act IV, Scene 1

About the Compiler

Steve King is a playwright and drama editor. His plays include *Incident, Yellow Lines, The Well-Made Life* and, most recently, a version of Hristo Boytchev's *The Titanic Orchestra* for the Edinburgh Fringe Festival, the largest international arts festival. Born in Aberdeen, Scotland, he now lives in London, England – the theatre capital of the world and home of Shakespeare's Globe Theatre.